P9-DNS-594

My First Book of
CHINESE WORDS
AN ABC RHYMING BOOK

Published by Tuttle Publishing, an imprint of Periplus Editions (HK) Ltd.

www.tuttlepublishing.com

Copyright © 2013 Text and Illustrations by Periplus Editions (HK) Ltd.

All rights reserved. No part of this publication may be reproduced or utilized in any form or by any means, electronic or mechanical, including photocopying, recording, or by any information storage and retrieval system, without prior written permission from the publisher.

Library of Congress Cataloging-in-Publication Data
Wu, Faye-Lynn.
My first book of Chinese words : an ABC rhyming book / by Faye-Lynn Wu
; illustrated by Aya Padrón.
    p. cm.
ISBN 978-0-8048-4367-6
1. Chinese language--Textbooks for foreign speakers--English--Juvenile
literature. 2. Chinese characters--Juvenile literature. I. Padrón, Aya,
ill. II. Title.
PL1129.E5W723 2012
495.1'82421--dc23

2012029068

ISBN 978-0-8048-4367-6

Distributed by

North America, Latin America & Europe
Tuttle Publishing
364 Innovation Drive, North Clarendon, VT 05759-9436 U.S.A.
Tel: 1 (802) 773-8930; Fax: 1 (802) 773-6993
info@tuttlepublishing.com; www.tuttlepublishing.com

Japan
Tuttle Publishing
Yaekari Building, 3rd Floor, 5-4-12 Osaki,
Shinagawa-ku, Tokyo 141 0032, Japan
Tel: (81) 3 5437-0171; Fax: (81) 3 5437-0755
sales@tuttle.co.jp; www.tuttle.co.jp

Asia Pacific
Berkeley Books Pte. Ltd.
61 Tai Seng Avenue # 02-12, Singapore 534167
Tel: (65) 6280-1330; Fax: (65) 6280-6290
inquiries@periplus.com.sg; www.periplus.com

Indonesia
PT Java Books Indonesia
Kawasan Industri Pulogadung
JI. Rawa Gelam IV No. 9, Jakarta 13930
Tel: (62) 21 4682-1088; Fax: (62) 21 461-0206
crm@periplus.co.id; www.periplus.com

First edition
17 16 15 14 13   10 9 8 7 6 5 4 3 2 1   1212TW

Printed in Malaysia

TUTTLE PUBLISHING® is a registered trademark of Tuttle Publishing, a division of Periplus Editions (HK) Ltd.

My First Book of
CHINESE WORDS
AN ABC RHYMING BOOK

BY FAYE-LYNN WU
ILLUSTRATED BY AYA PADRÓN

TUTTLE Publishing

Tokyo | Rutland, Vermont | Singapore

Dedication

Thank you to Mimi Gold and Siu-Mui Woo for
their guidance, and my siblings who helped create
the fun for my childhood memories.   F.W.

To Zoe.   A.P.

Preface

Similar to other Roman-based languages, the English language's phonetic and writing systems are tied together. Each letter in a word represents one of its sounds. Unlike English, Chinese writing is a pictographic system that evolved from pictures and symbols. The characters represent words and meanings, but not necessarily the sounds.

The goal of this book is to use playful rhymes and illustrations to introduce the Chinese language to young children. The words covered in this book include objects and actions that children across cultures are familiar with, such as body parts, moon, sun, saying goodbye, and words that specifically relate to the Chinese culture, such as bāozi (a Chinese snack food) and kuàizi (chopsticks).

You will see that each Chinese character is spelled in Pinyin, a phonetic sound system that uses Roman letters to transcribe the Chinese sounds. Pinyin assigns letters different sound values from those of English. For example:

c is pronounced as ts in "its"
ch is pronounced as ch in "chirp"
j is pronounced as j in "jeep"
q is pronounced as ch in "cheap"
x is pronounced as sh in "she"

r is pronounced as z in "azure"
sh is pronounced as sh in "shut"
z is pronounced as ds in " woods"
zh is pronounced as j in "jam"

To hear the Chinese words in this book spoken aloud, please visit this book's page at **www.tuttlepublishing.com**.

You'll also note that several of the words chosen are written in Traditional as well as Simplified characters.

Although Chinese differs greatly from English, it is a fun language to learn, and young children are ideal learners of new languages. We hope you'll enjoy sharing the Chinese language with your child through these fun rhymes.

爱 ┊ 愛

simplified | traditional

A is for *ài*,
a word that means love,
like the gentle hugs
that wrap us like the
soft wings of a dove.

6

包子

B is for *bāozi.*
A bun of soft dough
filled with tasty bits —
when it's hot eat it slow!

Bāozi is a traditional Chinese snack. It can be filled with meat or veggies, or with sweet bean paste. Yum!

茶

C is for *chá*,
a steaming cup of **tea**.
We all sit around the
table, and the cup is
passed from you to me.

Tea is the most common
drink among Chinese
people. It is enjoyed with
meals and snacks, and
also with company.

灯笼
simplified

D is for *dēnglóng*,
lantern hung up high—
a bright paper lamp
against the night sky.

燈籠
traditional

猜灯谜

Lanterns represent joy,
harmony, and good luck.
At Lantern Festival people
like to hang riddles from
them so their friends can
have fun guessing.

9

耳 **E** is for *ěr*.
This is your **ear**,
listening, listening—
what do you hear?

10

风
筝
simplified

風
筝
traditional

F is for *fēngzhēng*.
A kite soars in the sky
like a beautiful dancer,
swirls, twirls, waves goodbye.

It's said that the Chinese invented kites thousands of years ago!

狗

G is for *gǒu*.
Our **dog** very dear
gives a happy "wang wang!"
when friends come near.

Different people hear and describe
sounds differently. The Chinese
hear cats say *mee mee*, ducks say
gua gua, and cows say *mou mou*.
What do you hear?

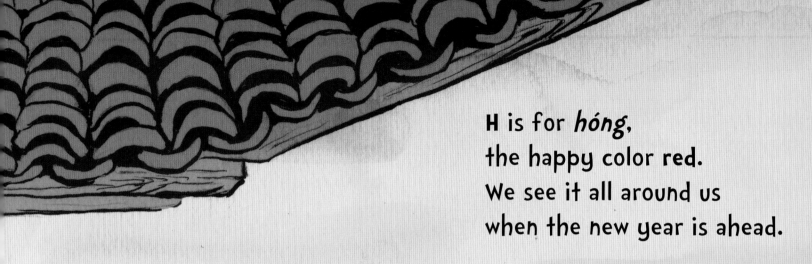

H is for *hóng*,
the happy color **red**.
We see it all around us
when the new year is ahead.

红 ┊ 紅

simplified ┊ traditional

The color red stands
for happiness.
It is usually used
to decorate when
festivals come
around, like Chinese
New Year and
weddings and many
other celebrations.

冰

I is for ice.
We call it *bing*.
It's cold in my mouth,
but then soon it's melting.

The letter **i** Chinese
sounds like e does in
English words like "bee"
and "feet." In pinyin,
i is always followed by
a consonant.

家

J is for *jiā*.
My home is my nest,
a place to return to—
that's where I rest.

筷子

K is for *kuàizi*, chopsticks—it takes two to bring yummy bites from your plate to you.

L is for _lóng_.
Dragon power is good.
With a big, mighty roar
dragon guards our
neighborhood.

龙
simplified

龍
traditional

In Chinese culture the dragon means
strength, generosity, and good luck.
In Chinese neighborhoods all over the
world the dragon dance celebrates
happy occasions.

17

米 M is for *mǐ*,
a bowl of cooked **rice**,
piled up high,
so steamy and nice.

Rice is a very important dish in
Chinese culture. Some families
like to eat it with every meal.

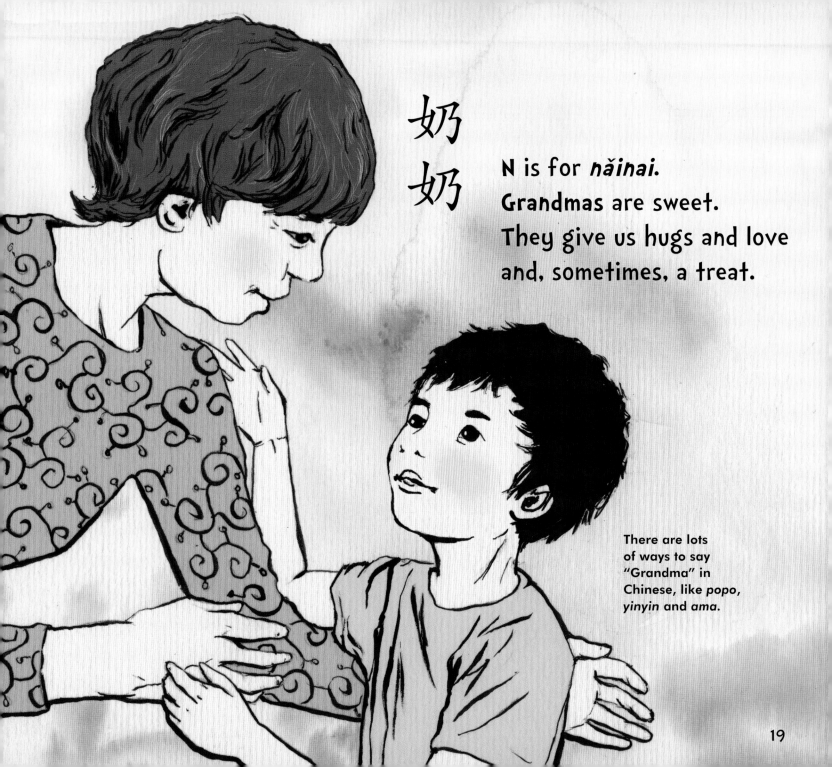

奶
奶

N is for *năinai*.
Grandmas are sweet.
They give us hugs and love
and, sometimes, a treat.

There are lots
of ways to say
"Grandma" in
Chinese, like *popo*,
yinyin and *ama*.

O is for *ōu*.
See how the gull flies.
Circling above,
"o-o I'm hungry!" he cries.

鸥 | 鷗

simplified | traditional

朋
友

P is for *péngyǒu*, the friends we see each day. Laughing, holding hands, together we play.

21

球 Q is for *qiú*.
A ball smooth and round
bounces high to the sky
and comes back to the ground.

日

R is for *rì*.
The bright, hot sun
with a shining
happy face says
"Get up! It's time
for fun!"

23

手 S is for *shǒu*.
What can your hands do?
They touch, count,
build, play—and
can tickle, too!

头 | 頭

simplified | traditional

T is for *tóu*.
Your wonderful **head**
lets you see, hear, smell, taste and talk,
and remember what is said.

雨伞
simplified

雨傘
traditional

U is for umbrella.
When rain falls from the sky
we need our *yǔsǎn*
to keep us dry.

In pinyin the letter u rhymes with the
English word "blue." This letter is
never used at the beginning of a word.

小提琴

V is for **violin**.
We call it *xǐaotíqín*.
Draw the bow over
the strings—
the xǐaotíqín sings!

Chinese doesn't have
a v sound but Chinese
culture has lots of
beautiful violin music.

尾巴

W is for *wěibā*.
A happy wagging **tail**
greets you with joy
day or night, without fail.

熊
猫

X is for *xióngmāo.*
Furry panda, soft as
sheep, munches on
bamboo leaves and
drifts off to sleep.

29

月

Y is for *yùe*.
The moon shines so bright.
Dancing with twinkling stars,
it lights up the dark night.

再见
simplified

再見
traditional

Z is for *zàijiàn.*
"Goodbye!" we say—
more good times together
when we meet another day.

Zài 再 means "again" and jiàn 见 means "see."
When the two words are put together they mean
"See you again!" which is how Chinese people
say "goodbye."

31

The Tuttle Story: "Books to Span the East and West"

Most people are surprised to learn that the world's largest publisher of books on Asia had its humble beginnings in the tiny American state of Vermont. The company's founder, Charles Tuttle, came from a New England family steeped in publishing, and his first love was books—especially old and rare editions.

Tuttle's father was a noted antiquarian dealer in Rutland, Vermont. Young Charles honed his knowledge of the trade working in the family bookstore, and later in the rare books section of Columbia University Library. His passion for beautiful books—old and new—never wavered throughout his long career as a bookseller and publisher.

After graduating from Harvard, Tuttle enlisted in the military and in 1945 was sent to Tokyo to work on General Douglas MacArthur's staff. He was tasked with helping to revive the Japanese publishing industry, which had been utterly devastated by the war. When his tour of duty was completed, he left the military, married a talented and beautiful singer, Reiko Chiba, and in 1948 began several successful business ventures.

To his astonishment, Tuttle discovered that postwar Tokyo was actually a book-lover's paradise. He befriended dealers in the Kanda district and began supplying rare Japanese editions to American libraries. He also imported American books to sell to the thousands of GIs stationed in Japan. By 1949, Tuttle's business was thriving, and he opened Tokyo's very first English-language bookstore in the Takashimaya Department Store in Ginza, to great success. Two years later, he began publishing books to fulfill the growing interest of foreigners in all things Asian.

Though a westerner, Tuttle was hugely instrumental in bringing a knowledge of Japan and Asia to a world hungry for information about the East. By the time of his death in 1993, he had published over 6,000 books on Asian culture, history and art—a legacy honored by Emperor Hirohito in 1983 with the "Order of the Sacred Treasure," the highest honor Japan bestows upon non-Japanese.

The Tuttle company today maintains an active backlist of some 1,500 titles, many of which have been continuously in print since the 1950s and 1960s—a great testament to Charles Tuttle's skill as a publisher. More than 60 years after its founding, Tuttle Publishing is more active today than at any time in its history, still inspired by Charles Tuttle's core mission—to publish fine books to span the East and West and provide a greater understanding of each.

DISCARD